BUILDING BLOCKS OF BIOLOGY

EVOLUTION

Written by William D. Adams

Illustrated by Ruth Bennett

www.worldbook.com

Co-published by agreement between Shi Tu Hui and World Book, Inc.

Shi Tu Hui
Room 1807, Block 1,
#3 West Dawang Road
Chaoyang District, Beijing 100025
P.R. China

World Book, Inc.
180 North LaSalle Street
Suite 900
Chicago, Illinois 60601
USA

© 2026. All rights reserved. This volume may not be reproduced in whole or in part in any form without prior written permission from the publisher.

WORLD BOOK and the GLOBE DEVICE are registered trademarks or trademarks of World Book, Inc.

Library of Congress Control Number: 2025942744

Building Blocks of Biology
ISBN: 978-0-7166-6737-7 (set, hard cover)

Evolution
ISBN: 978-0-7166-6747-6 (hard cover)

Also available as:
ISBN: 978-0-7166-6767-4 (e-book)
ISBN: 978-0-7166-6757-5 (soft cover)

WORLD BOOK STAFF

Editorial

Vice President
Tom Evans

Senior Manager, New Content
Jeff De La Rosa

Proofreader
Nathalie Strassheim

Graphics and Design

Senior Visual Communications Designer
Melanie Bender

Acknowledgments
Writer: William D. Adams
Illustrator: Ruth Bennett/The Bright Agency

TABLE OF CONTENTS

Family Trees 4

Last Common Ancestor 8

Natural Selection 12

Science Fun with Fur:
Simulating Selection 18

Extinction 20

Sexual Selection 26

Artificial Selection 30

Present Imperfect 32

Life on the Edge: De-Extinction 34

Show What You Know 38

Answers and Words to Know 40

There is a glossary on page 40. Terms defined in the glossary are in type **that looks like this** on their first appearance.

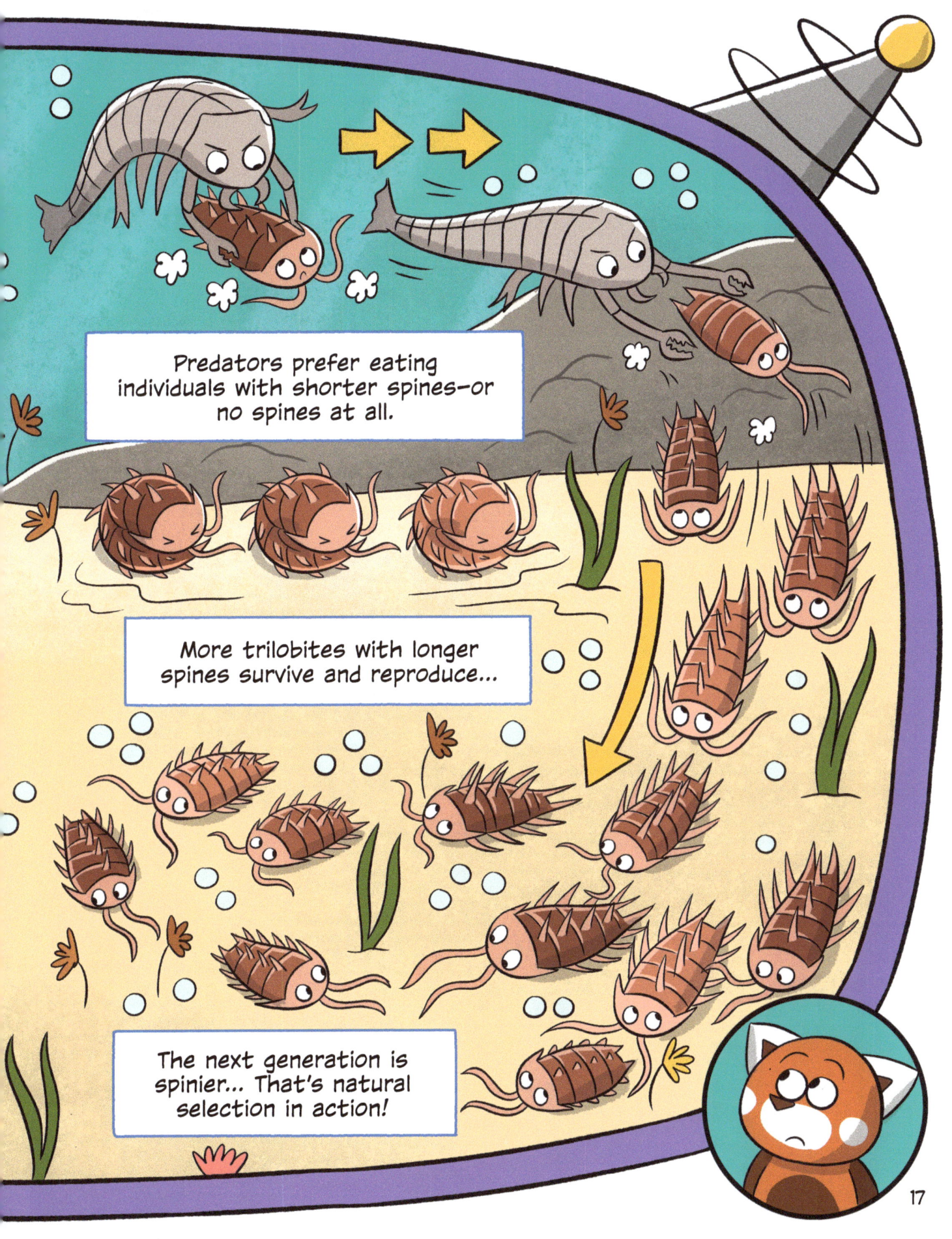

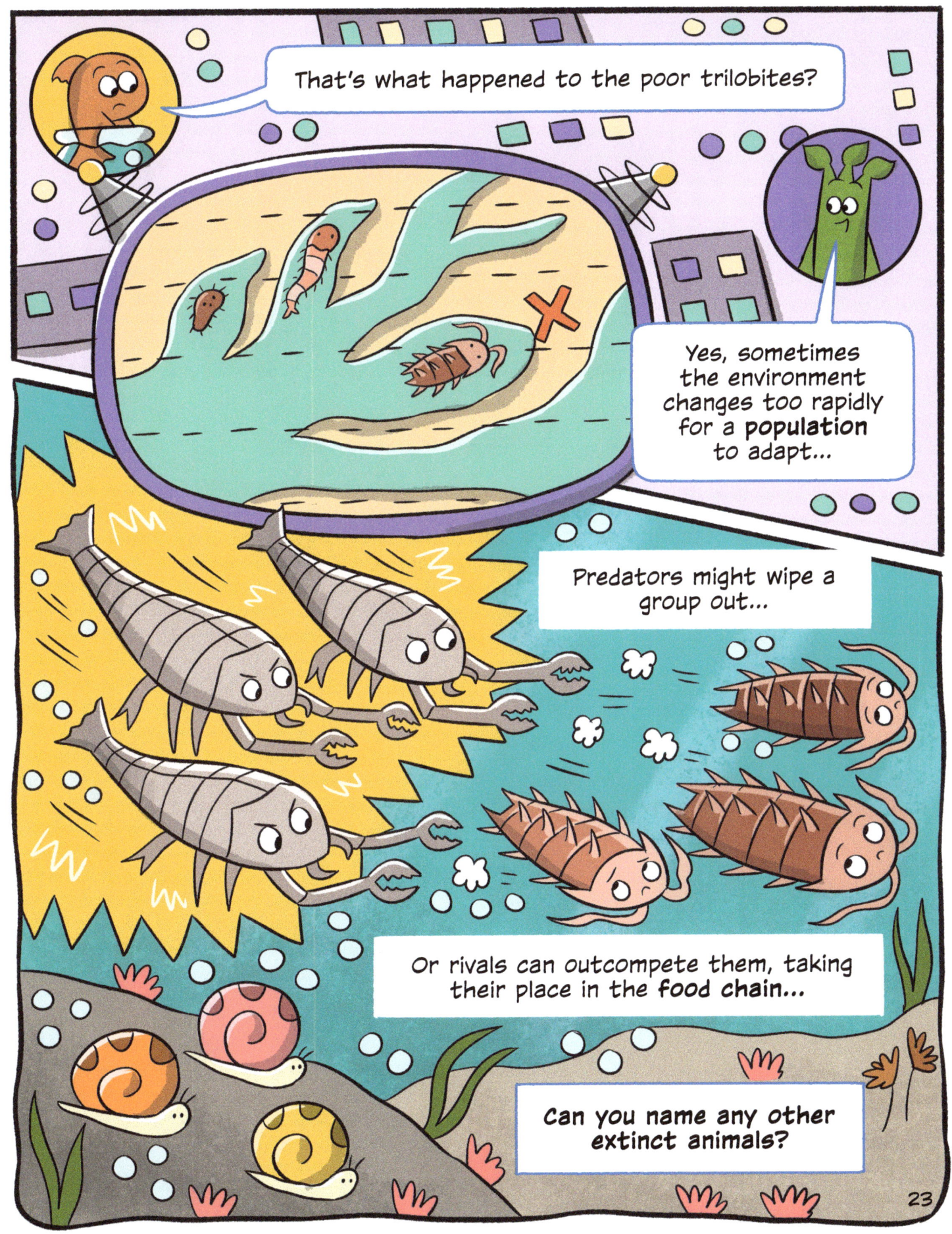

SHOW WHAT YOU KNOW

1. True or false?

   A. First cousins share about 50 percent of their genes.
   B. All offspring are identical to their parents.
   C. Living things inherit genes from their parents.

2. Match each word to its definition:

   evolution
   extinction
   heredity

   A. the process by which a living thing inherits characteristics from its parents
   B. the process by which a living thing develops over time
   C. the process by which a living thing dies out completely

3. Is each of the following true of artificial selection, natural selection, or sexual selection?

A. occurs when living things better suited to their environment survive and leave more offspring
B. occurs when living things select for certain traits through mating
C. occurs when people selectively breed animals for desirable characteristics
D. antler size in Irish elk is an example
E. the type of selection that resulted in modern dog breeds

4. Explain how trilobites might evolve to have longer spines through natural selection.

See page 40 for answers.

ANSWERS

page 9: 12.5 percent

page 27: sexual selection

SHOW WHAT YOU KNOW ANSWERS
pages 38-39:

1. A. false
   B. false
   C. true

2. A. heredity
   B. evolution
   C. extinction

3. A. natural selection
   B. sexual selection
   C. artificial selection
   D. sexual selection
   E. artificial selection

4. Longer spines help to protect trilobites from predators. Trilobites with longer spines survive to produce more offspring. Over time, longer spines thus become more common.

WORDS TO KNOW

artificial selection type of selection in which people breed living things with desirable characteristics.

DNA the molecule that encodes the genes of living things.

evolution the process by which living things change over time.

extinct died out completely.

first cousins family members whose parents are siblings.

food chain the process by which energy passes from one organism to another in the form of food.

genes the chemical units through which living things inherit their traits.

heredity the passing on of biological characteristics from one generation to the next.

intrasexual selection type of selection that occurs when living things compete for access to mates.

mutation a change in a gene.

natural selection the process by which living things better suited to their environment survive and produce more offspring.

population a particular group of living things.

predator a living thing that preys (feeds) on another living thing; hunting animal.

sexual selection type of selection influenced by the choice of mates for sexual reproduction.

species a single distinct kind of living thing.

www.ingramcontent.com/pod-product-compliance
Lightning Source LLC
Chambersburg PA
CBHW061256170426
43191CB00041B/2435